JAGDPANZER

Jagdpanzer IV · Jagdpanther

Horst Scheibert

Left: Jagdpanzer IV, first type, with the Pak 39 L/48 gun. It is now at the open-air museum of the Combat Troop School 2 of the Bundeswehr in Munster (Lüneburg Heath).

SCHIFFER MILITARY HISTORY
West Chester, PA

Photo Credits:
Federal Archives, Koblenz (BA)
Combat Troop School 2 of the Bundeswehr
Podzun Archives
Scheibert Archives

Translated from the German by Dr. Edward Force,
Central Connecticut State University.

Printed in the United States of America.
ISBN: 0-88740-323-9

This title was originally published under the title,
Jagdpanzer,
by Podzun-Pallas Verlag, Friedberg.

We are interested in hearing from authors with book ideas on related topics. We are also looking for good photographs in the military history area. We will copy your photos and credit you should your materials be used in a future Schiffer project.

Published by Schiffer Publishing, Ltd.
1469 Morstein Road
West Chester, Pennsylvania 19380
Please write for a free catalog.
This book may be purchased from the publisher.
Please include $2.00 postage.
Try your bookstore first.

This is an early production Jagdpanzer IV with a Pak 39 gun. Interesting features include the Zimmerite covering and the round shields in front of the loopholes for defensive weapons. Later versions had just one of these, at the right side of the gun.

Jagdpanzer

As a response to the increasingly numerous tanks of the Allies — opposed to the 25,000 tanks of the Axis Powers there were almost 250,000 of the Allies — Germany developed a number of tank destroyers, from improvised types to the Jagdtiger, the strongest armored weapon of World War II.

Above: This Jagdpanzer IV was in a village on the Vistula in the winter of 1944-45.

Right: Drawing of the first version of Jagdpanzer IV (also called Panzerjäger 39 after its Pak 39 gun). It can be recognized by the short gun with muzzle brake.

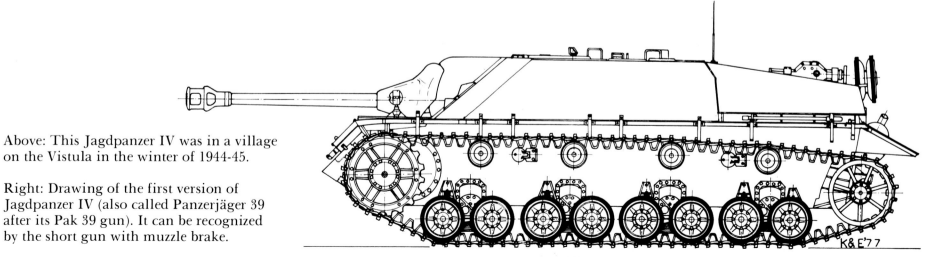

Jagdpanzer IV

At the time it was appropriate to build a tank destroyer on the Panzer IV chassis. That of Type H was generally used for this purpose. Along with Assault Gun IV — basically a tank destroyer too — there were five more or less different versions:

Prototype built by the VOMAG Works
With 75mm Pak 39 L/48 (also called Panzerjäger 39), Sd.Kfz. 162
With 75mm KwK 42 L/70, Sd.Kfz. 162/1 (with four return rollers)
The same vehicle with only three return rollers, and
With 75mm Stuk. 42 L/70, Sd.Kfz. 162/2. This version, unlike those above, still had the upper part of the Panzer IV hull.

Most Panzerjäger 39 and Jagdpanzer IV were built with only three return rollers.

Since the Pak 39 L/48 did not offer any improvement over the Assault Gun III in terms of weaponry, the more expensive chassis of the Panzer IV was an extravagance. The installation of the better gun of the Panther (KwK 42, L/70) certainly improved the weapon performance, but the heavy cannon put so much weight on the front end that the Panzerjäger's shooting precision and handling characteristics suffered.

These pictures show a prototype of the Jagdpanzer IV made by VOMAG. This vehicle also has two round shields over loopholes for short-range defense.

Left: This photo shows the first production version of Jagdpanzer IV with a somewhat more inclined front plate and the usual "pig's-head" mantelet commonly used with assault guns. This vehicle is now at the Aberdeen Tank Museum, USA.

Right: A Jagdpanzer IV of the same type — with a Panther behind it. The hooks on the edge of the track covers were provided to hang aprons on.

Left: The rear of a Jagdpanzer IV with partial Zimmerite covering (to prevent the adhesion of magnetic mines). For additional protection, the additional track links were hung on. The muffler was mounted transversely on two brackets.

Right: This is how the rear of the Jagdpanzer IV now at Munster looks. The Zimmerite covering and the muffler are missing, and some of the service openings are welded shut. The chassis — like almost all Panzerjäger 39's — is that of the Panzer IV Type H.

Above: This photo shows clearly how the round shields were pushed aside to free the loopholes for defensive weapons. They turn on an axis on the right side of the opening. For this reason there was no Zimmerite covering.

Upper right: Here is a front view, and . . .

Right: . . . another rear view. The antenna (right rear) is easy to see. The soldiers sitting on it have just received the latest field newspaper.

A Jagdpanzer IV with its 75mm Pak 39 L/48 gun, aprons and Zimmerite covering.

A Panzerjäger 39 without aprons or a muzzle brake.

These and the following photos show details of the Jagdpanzer IV now at Combat Troop School 2 of the Bundeswehr in Munster.

Right: This tank differs from that just shown in that it lacks a loophole over the driver's visor to the left of the gun, a version also seen in later types.

The information on the sign is incorrect. It does not have a 75mm KwK 42 L/70, but a Pak 39 L/48 gun.

Unfortunately, an incorrect camouflage paint job.

14

Here are three more photos of the Panzerjäger 39.

At upper left it is seen in action; above is the vehicle at Munster, and at left a bird's-eye view. Here the entry hatches and the cutout for the aiming optics can be seen. It exists in almost the same form as on the Hetzer and Jagdpanther.

Some 1500 of the Panzerjäger 39 were probably built.

Above: A type not easily identified; the raised exhaust pipes could be a makeshift replacement for a missing muffler. The photo was taken in January of 1945.

Right: Two photos of the same Jagdpanzer IV of the 116th Panzer (Windhund) Division. It is one of the later types, recognizable by its lack of an opening over the driver's visor. The gun is somewhat confusing; by the short barrel, it must be a Pak 39, but it lacks a muzzle brake.(BA)

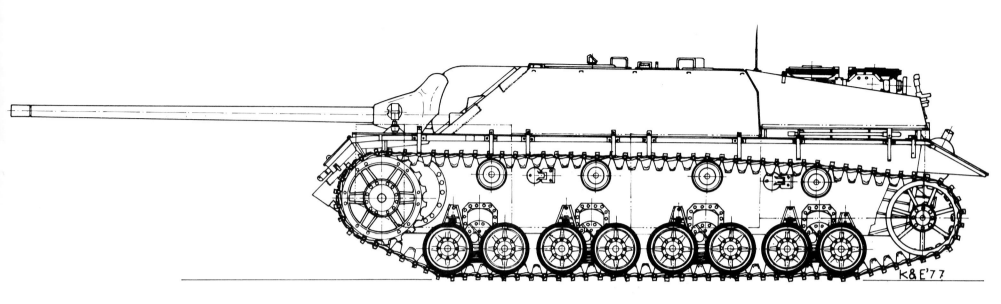

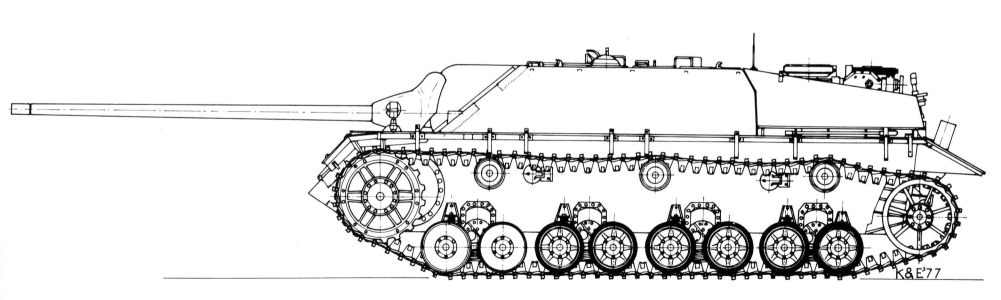

The two versions with the longer L/70 75mm KwK (the Panther) differ in having four (rarely) and three return rollers and different road wheels (all still with rubber wrappings or partly (usually in front) steel wheels.

18

A Jagdpanzer IV, Sd.Kfz. 162/1 L/70, with four return rollers. The engine covers are opened, the rear side armor and aprons are missing.

Here is a Jagdpanzer IV with only three return rollers, but it also has rubber wrappings on all the road wheels.

Here are two pictures of Jagdpanzer IV L/70 with aprons. The number of return rollers cannot be seen, but both still have rubber on all their road wheels.

Above: A wrecked Jagdpanzer IV near Dreierwalde. The number 221 shows that it was the platoon leader's vehicle of the 2nd platoon of the 2nd company.

Right photos: Shown is a Jagdpanzer IV with three return rollers and four steel forward road wheels. In the upper picture the bracket needed to hold the long gun barrel (while marching) can be seen.

A Jagdpanzer IV of later type with "light and shadow camouflage paint." The shear telescope is easy to see. It shows only three return rollers, but lacks aprons which, since they only hang in place (note the hooks for them on the track cover), were easily lost.

Above: A look into the fighting compartment (after removal of the roof armor). The upper wheel is for the gun's elevation, the lower one for traverse.

Upper right: A look at the driver's seat (removed). At right is the motor, over it a diagram that shows one reverse and six forward speeds.

Right: In this drawing, the steel disc that covers the close-combat loophole can be seen to the right of the gun.

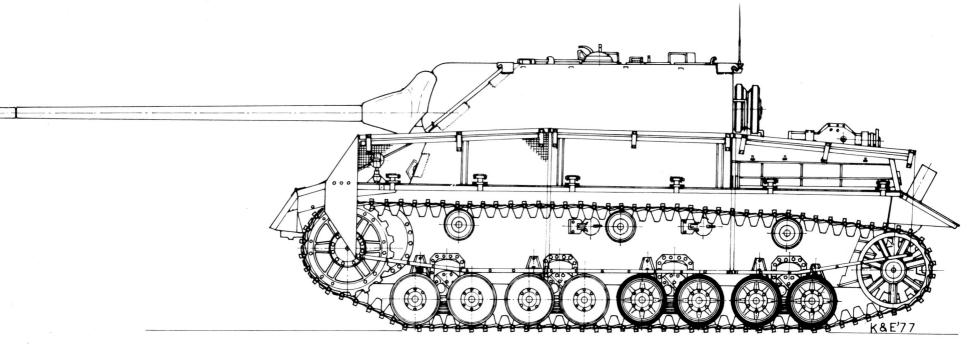

Above: The Jagdpanzer IV L/70 on the chassis of Panzer IV with the higher hull — very few of these were made.

Right: Unlike the previous Jagdpanzer IV, this one has the typical Panzer IV bow. It could thus be classified as an Assault Gun IV (Sturmgeschütz), yet it has the Panther gun, as do the Jagdpanzer shown before.

Jagdpanzer IV
mit 7,5 cm KwK 42
L/70

24

While the picture on the previous page shows no gun bracket on the bow, it can be seen in these three photos.

It is also noteworthy in the left photo that the four forward road wheels (unlike those in the picture on the previous page) are steel wheels, and in the picture below, a machine gun can be seen in the close-combat loophole. All three photos were taken in the spring of 1945 on German soil, the lower two south of Bad Kreuznach.

Jagdpanther - Jagdpanzer V

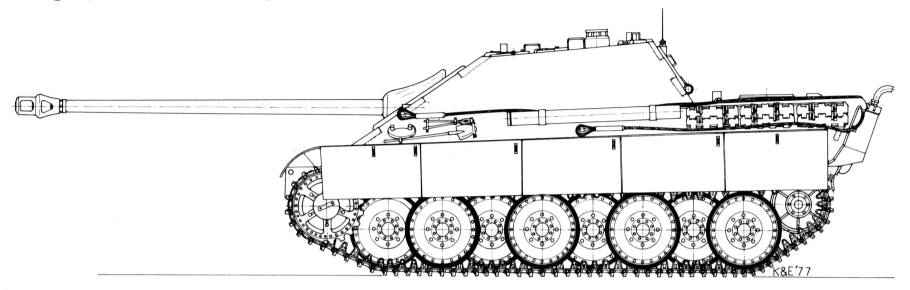

The earlier version with the one-piece gun
barrel.

The later version of Sd.Kfz. 173, the type
usually built.

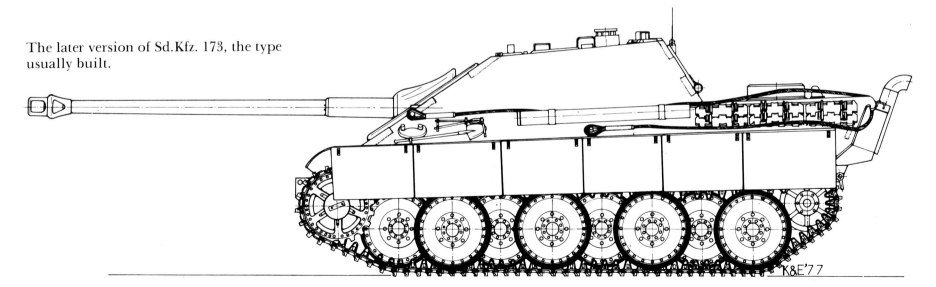

Jagdpanther (Jagdpanzer V)

Since the superb 75mm KwK L/70 was not practical on the Jagdpanzer IV chassis, it was necessary to build the Jagdpanzer V, also called the Jagdpanther. It usually lacked a rotating turret and its silhouette was some 23.5 cm lower than that of the Panther. It was more heavily armored than all previously built Jagdpanzer and was exceeded only by the Jagdtiger. Its versions vary only in minor details:
Different exhaust systems
Different mantelets, and
With a one- or two-piece Pak 43 gun.

It ranked among the best tank destroyers on World War II. It blended heavy armor and a low silhouette with the effect of the good 88mm Pak. In all, 382 of them were built.

Here is the one-piece cannon. Below and on the opposite page is the later version; it made changing the barrel easier.(3 x BA)

A look into the fighting compartment with the rear visor, ammunition (at the side), and part of the gun mount. The space is relatively large.

Above: Here again, two versions can be recognized. The two front views also show another difference: compared to the earlier type, the later one has only a one-piece driver's visor.

Right: Maneuvers in France before the 1944 invasion; the rear entry port is easy to see.(2 x BA)

Unlike the Panther, it had an 88mm Pak, which gave it the firepower of a Tiger.(BA)

These three photos show the Jagdpanther at Combat Troop School 2 of the Bundeswehr in Munster. Some of the outer road wheels are missing, and others are mounted too high, thus its unfortunate position. But it affords the possibility of taking detailed photos (see next pages).

Jagdpanzer V (Fahrgest.
Panther)
1944
Kanone 8,8 L 71
Gew: 46 t PS: 600
Besatzung: 5

Here again are two pictures from France, summer 1944.(2 x BA)

Right page: Pictures of the Jagdpanther at the open-air museum in Munster. The later, stronger loophole covers are easy to see.

This page: This Jagdpanther at the open-air museum in Aberdeen, Maryland, also shows the heavier loophole shield.

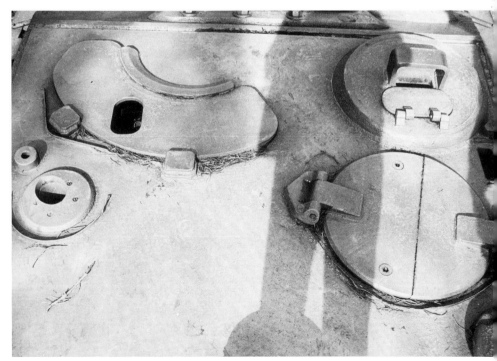

Above: The stern of the machine at Munster,

Left: The roof of Sd.Kfz. 173; the two round diagonally arranged entry ports, the three periscopes (here removed) protected by arched bars, the ventilator (center) and at the left front, the cutout for the aiming optics. This can be seen in similar form in the Jagdpanzer IV and the Hetzer.

Driving in a row across a drill field in France, 1944.

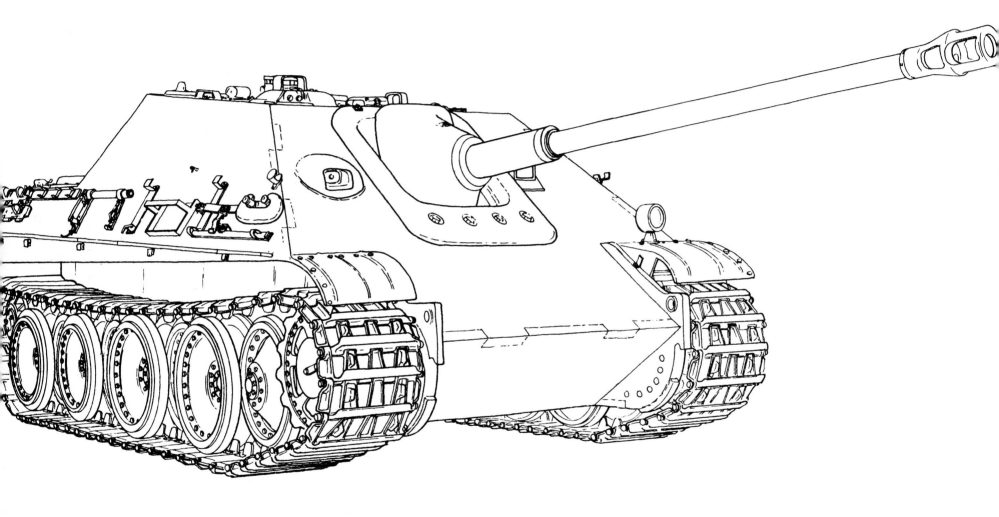

Upper right: The Zimmerite covering is easy to see here. The soldier is spraying the machine with camouflage paint.

Above and right: It is interesting that this gun needed no marching bracket. The picture above again shows the earlier model with the one-piece gun.

The blend of a low silhouette with the good 88mm gun and heavier armor in shell-deflecting shapes produced an optimal tank for its time — probably the best Jagdpanzer ever.(2 x BA)

Left: Jagdpanther that fell into Allied hands — mostly in France, Belgium, Holland and western Germany! Most of them were not lost in battle, but for lack of fuel, or were left in enemy hands by their crews when the war ended.

Technical Data

Jagdpanzer IV
Panzerjäger 39

Motor:	Maybach HL 120 TRM
Cylinders:	12 (60-degree V)
Bore x stroke:	105 x 115 mm
Displacement:	11867 cc
Maximum power:	300 HP at 3000 rpm
Sustained power:	265 HP at 2600 rpm
Compression ratio:	1 : 6.5
Carboretors:	2 Solex 40 JFF H two-stage cross-country downdraft
Valves:	Dropped, 1 camshaft per cylinder head, gear-driven
Crankshaft bearings:	7; changeable cylinder liners
Cooling:	Water-cooled with pump
Battery:	4 x 12-volt, 105 Ah
Generator:	600 Watt
Starter:	4 HP
Power transmission:	Rear engine, drive to track running gear, three-plate clutch
Gearbox:	ZF Aphon SDSG 77, 6 forward speeds, 1 reverse, 2nd to 6th gears synchro mesh
Differential:	Spur gear system, 3.23 ratio
Body:	Self-carrying armored hull, armored superstructure without rotating turret
Running gear:	2 tracks of 99 links each, drive wheel forward, steering wheel aft, 8 small double road wheels in rows, 4 return rollers, as of 1945 3 return rollers, 4 quarter springs (1 per pair of road wheels)
Steering and braking:	Mechanical planetary steering gear and mechanical steering brakes, 2 steering levers

General data:

Track length:	3520 mm
Track of vehicle:	2450 mm
Track width:	400 mm
Overall dimensions:	5900 x 3170 x 1860 mm
with gun:	6850 x 3170 x 1860 mm
Armor:	Front 60 mm, sides 40 mm, rear 30 mm
Ground clearance:	400 mm
Fording ability:	1000 mm
Turning circle:	6 meters
Total weight:	24,000 kg
Load limit:	1500 kg
Top speed:	40 kph
Fuel consumption per 100 km:	Road 240, off-road 360 liters
Fuel capacity:	470 liters
Range:	Road 190, off-road 130 km
Crew:	4 or 5 men
Armament:	75mm Pak L/48 + 1 machine gun

Jagdpanzer

Motor:	Maybach HL 230 P 30
Cylinders:	12 (60-degree V)
Bore x stroke:	130 x 145 mm
Displacement:	23,800 cc
Maximum power:	700 HP at 3000 rpm
Sustained power:	600 HP at 2500 rpm
Compression ratio:	1 : 6.8
Carburetors:	4 Solex 52 JFF II D double downdraft cross-country
Valves:	Dropped, 1 camshaft per cylinder head, gear-driven
Crankshaft bearings:	8; changeable cylinder liners
Cooling:	Water-cooled with pump
Battery:	2 12-volt, 120 or 150 Ah
Generator:	700 Watt
Starter:	6 HP
Power transmission:	Rear engine, drive to track running gear, three-plate dry clutch
Gearbox:	ZF Synchron AK 7-400, 7 forward speeds, 1 reverse, 2nd to 7th gears synchro mesh
Differential:	Spur-gear system, ratio 8.4
Body:	Self-carrying armored superstructure, no rotating turret
Running gear:	2 tracks of 86 links each, drive wheel forward, steering wheel aft, 8 large double road wheels in pairs, 2 suspension members per wheel pair
Steering and braking:	Hydraulic steering gear, drive wheels with hydraulic Argus disc brakes

General data:

Track length:	3900 mm
Track of vehicle:	2620 mm
Track width:	660 mm
Overall dimensions:	6870 x 3270 x 2715 mm,
with gun and aprons:	9860 x 3420 x 2715 mm
Armor:	Front 80 mm, sides and rear 40 to 50 mm
Ground clearance:	540 mm
Fording ability:	1550 mm
Turning circle:	10 meters
Allowable gross weight:	46,000 kg
Top speed:	46 kph
Fuel consumption/100 km:	Road 460, off-road 690 liters
Fuel capacity:	700 liters
Range:	Road 150, off-road 100 km
Crew:	5 men
Armament:	88mm Pak L/71 + 1 machine gun

AFTERWORD

From a combat point of view, the way of using chassis of the heavier battle tanks IV, V and VI to build tank destroyers was a mistake and an extravagance. Heavy armor was and is not so important for a tank destroyer; protection against shrapnel and handguns is sufficient. More important are a robust, proven powerplant, a low silhouette, great mobility and a strong, long-range weapon. Today these demands are met by a Jeep with a two-man crew and a long-range self-targeting rocket.

Seen in this light — if its height is not considered — the Rhinoceros tank destroyer with its well-developed chassis, larger fighting compartment and very good 88mm Pak came nearest to being optimal at the time. Because of its very low silhouette, the Hetzer was also very favorable but had a very cramped fighting compartment. Between the two were the Marder II and III. The best "Panzerjäger", though, proved to be the Sturmgeschütz III, and it was not by chance that this machine scored the highest numbers of kills of enemy tanks. It was not classed as a tank destroyer, and yet it was the best. Symptomatic of this fact was the equipping of many Panzerjäger units with them.

The path to more and more heavily armored vehicles of World War II was necessary for offensive weapons, but not for the tank destroyers that stood and waited for their targets.

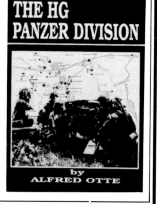